To be Nonchalantly Alive

To be Nonchalantly Alive

Poems by

Kerry Trautman

Cover design by Shay Culligan

Cover photograph by Adrian Lime

ISBN: 978-1-952326-13-4

Kelsay Books
502 South 1040 East, A-119
American Fork, Utah, 84003

This book is dedicated to those in the Ohio poetry community who have provided feedback, friendship and encouragement over the years, especially Joel Lipman, the late Marianna Hofer, and my beloved Almeda Street Poets: Michael Hackney, Michael Kocinski, Adrian Lime, Jonie McIntire, Lori Nikoli-Kuykendall, and the late John Swaile.

Acknowledgments

The author would like to thank the publications in which some of the poems in this collection previously appeared:

"Boat Trip" *Tuesday Nights at Sam & Andy's Uptown Café* (Westron Press 2001); "Banana Aubade" *Alimentum* (2007); "Food for the Dead" *Broadway Bards First* (The Poetry Barn Press 2010); and *Bards Again* (The Poetry Barn Press 2016); "The Table" Judd's Hill Winery website (2011); "Jeanne Calment of France" *Mock Turtle Zine* (2012); "Los Angeles Hotel Breakfast" *Mixolydian Blues* (2013); "The Argyle Building Fire" *Naugatuck River Review* (2013); "To the Roofers" *The Madison Review* (2014);"To the Brass Safety Pin" *Five2One* (2015); "To the Poets" and "Toast and Coffee" www.toledopoet.com (2015); "Florist Fire" and "To JM, Creative Writing 301" *Common Threads* (Ohio Poetry Association Press 2015); "Beta Fish" *The Toledo Streets Anthology* (2016); "Cardamom" *The Fourth River* (2016); "Of Oils" *After Happy Hour Review* (2016); "Luck," "Cycles ," and "A Taste for Salt" *Five2One* (2016); "What Ohio Needs" *Fourth & Sycamore* (2016); "Daylong June Downpour" *Common Threads* (Ohio Poetry Association Press 2016); "Soot," "Coney Island," and "Without Blue" *Mock Turtle Zine* (2017); "June Cherry-Picking Pantoum" *Ohio Poetry Day Awards Anthology* (Ohio Poetry Day Press 2017); "I've Never Been to Cleveland" *US 20 Poetry Anthology* (Foothills Publishing 2018); "Wisdom" and "Roasting Turkey for Friends" *Gasconade Review: Gas Station Famous* (2018); "To the Pineapple" *Mock Turtle Zine* (2018); "Fifteen Minutes" *Slippery Elm* (2019).

Contents

Cardamom

Tell me—
does it taste like the glow of marigolds
strung along a white wedding tent?

Does it taste like a heel of pulla bread
slipped in my great grandmother's wool
coat pocket as she boarded a ship
in Helsinki, bound eventually for
Michigan's Upper Peninsula?

Does it taste green?
Or like white blossoms
streaked fuchsia, or like
rhizomes sprung ground-level from
upright sprays of leaves?

Does it taste both warm and cooling,
like a balm for tubercular lungs?
Does it elicit a promise of calm?

To the Cousins

It is as if you never knew—those summers
riding bicycles through campgrounds to the beach,
returning by dusk for the fire, blackened
marshmallows stuck to each other's lips
and fingertips and hair, as if
everything would be joined sweetly forever.
It is as if you thought you would be girls always,
and never women, mothers. Girls
fantasizing about being sisters,
lamenting the real ones,
blood enough to love Shakespearian, then
say goodbye for months at a time,
giggling into purple pen-pal ink
and scratch-n-sniff stickers,
reunited at the whim of the mothers.
It is as if those lake breezes that whipped
your smoke-dried hair like damp snakes
across sunblindedness would still themselves
or not—it was not up to you.

What Ohio Needs

Ohio needs its northern shallow shores—
waves glinting at gulls and sandy toddlers.
Its inland lakes stocked with walleye,
pedalboats and water skis.
Waters busy and rushed from fishy April
through 'til winds of autumn,
stoically shoved grey with ice in February.

Ohio needs its southern hillsides—
rocky prelude to the Appalachians,
heaving cloaks of golden locust trees
and flaming maples, lush firs
stubbornly green against October.

Ohio needs its windswept fields—
churned and sowed dirt ruts,
skeletal irrigation apparatus towering overhead,
spewing spray on sun-cracked clay.
Its acres bursting with watched and waited-for
corn, soybeans, and winter wheat
with its gleaming emerald carpets.

Ohio needs its men—
nailbeds stained of earth, of motor oil,
of oil paints or newsprint.
Its men who sell freezers, Jeeps, antique settees.
Who x-ray molars, draw blood into vials,
or stand hours on factory lines, assembling
carburetors or boxes of bright lollipops.
Who shout at ball players and referees,
who drive too fast over winding highways,
windows down, mumbling along to
Garth Brooks, REM, or Zeppelin.
Who fix storm-wrenched fences

15

with what's shelved in their garages,
who kill snakes with shovels, nap with dogs,
stack charcoal on the backyard grill,
plucking which nearby tomato is reddest.

Ohio needs its women—
shoveling snow, casting for catfish off piers,
bathing fresh peach off their babies in sinks.
Its women who paint their fingernails, then
plunge them into yeasty dough or garden soil.
Who hang drapes to blacken themselves in
against winter frost and summer lightning.
Who tune weather radios, watch red-blotch
radars, shuttle young ones to the cellar.
Who teach, and doctor each other's children,
who hover over swivel chairs in cubicles in
semi-tall office towers studding grid streets.
Who reach to library stacks for Danielle Steel
or Davids Mamet or Sedaris.

Ohio needs its neighbors—
sharing overabundant zucchini, wax beans.
Neighbors who coach baseball on Saturdays that
start with mittens and end with shorts.
Who borrow lawn mowers or eggs,
drive carpools to brick schools,
help move a new sofa inside,
or flood-soaked carpeting out.
Who dole candy to costumed children,
haggle over yard-sale candlesticks and sweaters.
Who welcome newborns with balloons,
or offer pumpkin bread or plates of cheese
for the deaths of elderly mothers.

Ohio needs its children—
climbing crabapple boughs, selling red Kool-Aid,
reading the funnies at the kitchen table.
Children who sort Easter jellybeans by colors,
chucking the black ones into the thawing creek.
Who sing on their swings and bicycles,
work puzzles with uncles,
mimic their fathers' golf swing or their mothers'
sowing of marigold seeds.
Who pore over college offerings,
choosing one near enough to drive home.
Who learn to smoke from older brothers,
then quit for girlfriends.
Who build and destroy sandcastles,
dangle crayfish at shrieking sisters,
hurl themselves into flocks of gulls until
they alight, wailing, in a grey-white flurry,
dropping a feather or two or three.

To the Pineapple

You are unwelcome in Ohio August
with our farmer's markets—
fat melons, bellies yellowed from hot soil,
raspberry quarts oozing to cardtables,
red plums blushed gold—
unbelieving they came from nearby yards.
Who should be so lucky?

Whose back yard were you hacked
from? Some kid's machete whacking
your stalk, hefting the angry
wad of you inside to lose half of yourself
to the cutting board.

Our pears shape themselves to fit
palms, eaten whole on the drive home,
dripping sweaty t-shirts.

Fruits here are compliant wives yielding
themselves to touch. Red Haven peach
skin, smooth Winesaps, cherries near
bursting like water balloons,
blackberries juicing fingertips and
thighs squeezed between rows.

You make a chore of yourself—
leaf blades slit like paper cuts,
spiked welted skin, touch of
mold always in the nook of your bottom,
inedible fibrous spine,
brown bristle eyes embedded in
what's good of you.

Why would you come here in August
when Ohio fields orgasm into baskets?
Come back, maybe, in December
for a salad with pomegranate pips
and crisp plasticky starfruit,
when we have nothing real of our own.

Fifteen Minutes

(the Hartford Circus Fire, 7/6/1944)

Even the greatest showpieces on
earth are flammable. Pink tutus strapped around

elephant hides by muscled trainers.
Even their biceps and suspenders.

Even a proboscis
and feathered headdress,

and the five lions perched
up and over a steel arch.

Even the aerialists,
their sequined leotards, the whips

and chairs of tiger-tamers,
the high-wire unicycles, ballet slippers,

the ringmaster's top hat
and silk tail-coat.

Even the clowns painting
themselves in the dressing tent, craning

grease-painted ears toward a chorus
of chaos, lifting the lower canvas

flap to see stories-high flames and black
peanut-tiger-popcorn smoke.

Especially the 120-ton
big-top tent rain-proofed with gasoline

and paraffin which melts and
showers incinerating droplets to wooden

bleachers and collapsing tree-trunk
posts. Even the parents,

even as they scream themselves back into
smokeclouds of bursting balloons

and candy apples dragging
small, screaming, blackened

bodies to finish smoldering in
summer sun.

167 charred bodies stacked in mud, dressed
in what's left of sooty Sunday Best.

Zebras and giraffes stomping in the menagerie
tent smelling what's coming.

Two

Two bites until I knew
       I did not like persimmon.

Two halves of fruit
       on the countertop,
two spoons—
       one for me, one for my mother

scooping into luminescent flesh
       rind cups for orange doses.
Her two eyes offering.
My two feet on the kitchen tiles.

Two light sources in the room—
       the evening TV news and
       the Christmas tree.

Two fruits nearby
       I'd rather eat—
              Granny Smith apple,
              tangerine—
both in bowls-full beside
       the coffee machine.
Both juicier than
       the fuzzy persimmon—
              like a swallow of carpet.

Two more mouthfuls. Trying.
Like two other tastes combined—
       pear-scented soap,
       and pumpkin.
Two textures—
       Styrofoam and wax.

Her spoon in and up again.
Me, wishing I'd found
      what she did.

Two other children upstairs
      who refused to taste.

My two hands on the countertop.
Two spoons.

Toast and Coffee

1.

The boy licked butter from
his toast—half burnt—
and he nibbled
the best of it, because
she had put down
her mug and newspaper
to make it
and because
the butter and knife,
and plate were already
waiting on the counter
when he
shrugged downstairs.

2.

The air smelled like toast—
like a Thursday morning
before school
with coffee brewing,
and though he didn't
drink coffee yet,
its smell and the toast
at resilient dawn
were the walls themselves,
and he wanted for her
an endless pot.

3.

He made toast
for his mother
when she was too sick
for much else
and taught himself
the important lesson
of how to brew coffee.

Orion

Passers-by call the child *hero* now
that his mother is finally dead after months
of knowing it soon would be so.

But he is no more a hero than a plastic bowl
becomes *boat* when flood waters rise under it.

He refuses to eat tomatoes from the grocery.

His mother had hosed her plants,
alternately spraying him—
tomato, boy, tomato, boy, tomato.

He tasted hosewater in each salted slice.

His bedroom ceiling floats miles upward towards
something up there he's heard called Orion,
while his floor sinks toward China,

and he imagines if he grips his top sheet in his fists
while also counting as high as he can,
while also praying, while also searching for a star
in the gap between his curtains,

while also remembering the sound of her
dress-heeled shoes walking in the kitchen door, home,
then maybe, just maybe, daylight would
appear, and birdsong.

Wisdom

(after a mixed media painting by Randy Bennett)

St. Apollonia[1],
my daughter's jaw needs your wisdom
this morning, four teeth jerked away
as crows cawed outside
the oral surgeon's window.

Things will be taken from her
over and over again.
There aren't feathers enough to
embellish this knowledge.

St. Thomas Aquinas[2],
our schoolchildren need your robes
to shield them at their desks.
Buzzards soar above their jungle gyms,
sniffing for gunpowder.

There are always talons poised to uproot
tender feet from soil.

St. Luke the Evangelical[3],
take Apollonia's hand,
deflect the light, so my girl
cannot walk toward it.
Assure her there is nothing there to see.
That her regular Friday is worth finishing.

My daughter's physics teacher drew
diagrams of birds' wings and loft,
of levers and wedges and
the arcs of projectiles.

St. Gabriel Possenti[4],
lower any barrels raised at living targets,
intercede between flesh and lead,
alter trajectories.

Greyblack shadows hover circles over
calculus class and biology and
a Tuesday morning ACT administration.

Second-grade teachers are skilled at
pulling baby teeth.
Older, we dream our teeth fall out,
wake to dried drool on our cheek,
licking the rows to check
they're each accounted-for.

St. Dymphna[5],
relax troubled psyches.
Numb triggers and their fingers.

My girl will rest the weekend away
with pain pills, ice cream, and tv.

St. Raphael[6],
you're overwhelmed.
Beg the aid of blue-jays and goldfinches
like Sleeping Beauty might.
Make prisms from what pinpoints
of light you find in our dark.

Notes
[1] St. Apollonia is the patron saint of dentists.
[2] St. Thomas Aquinas is the patron saint of students.
[3] St. Luke the Evangelical is the patron saint of surgeons and artists.
[4] St. Gabriel Possenti is the patron saint of gun owners.
[5] St. Dymphna is the patron saint of mental illness.
[6] St. Raphael is the patron saint of doctors and pharmacists.

Sunday, Noon, Late December 2015

The church bells clamber over one another,
unable to decide a tune, instead insisting
themselves haphazardly into muddy sky—
refusing, so far this season, to snow.

A chain ting-tings against a flagpole with no flag,
not even at half-mast like all the others—
raised for a day, then re-lowered after the new
mass-shooting to make the news.

Perhaps we should take them all down,
fold them solemnly, up off the ground like
Boy Scouts do, like a woman
un-pinning Sunday laundry from the line,
folding a windy white bedsheet against
her chest in a sort of surrender.

To the Brass Safety Pin

You wait for fingertips,
tiny coil
a cold muscle
tensing the point
within its protective sheath.

Abandoned to a drawer or purse,
point exposed—
an exhibitionist awaiting
discovery,
a flinch and
the suck suck suck of
a punctured fingerpad.

You will be restrained again,
craving again release,
the opportunity to pierce,
to hold
not to be held.

Boat Trip

(8/29/2000)

All us poetry types
in a great little chartered boat,
with droplets of Maumee River mudwater
sprinkled on spiderwebs
glowing gold in anti-bug bulbs
swarmed with skeeters, gnats, and flies.
High on nighttime breeze
and borrowed perfect warm redwine
from a red plastic cup, and talk
of Kerouac and love and words and things.
I watched seagulls bouncefloat asleep
on wake ripplewaves,
little featherbody boats
there doin all the time
me only just now noticing,
and the boat—
rumba splosh
rumba splosh
rumba splosh

We docked on Little Sister Island,
mine just happening to be with me,
now hugging up on my neck saying
little sister love,
pushing me high on a treeswing there,
only hemp rope knotted through
a rough wood plank,
probably years-old dockwood
probably smelling dirt seaweed good
there under my thighs,

like the rope living with years of
fish-hands and smoke-hands
and Frisbee-in-the-sand hands
and swinging my hair did wave and whirl.
And folks partying there,
fires and bottles and smoke,
borrowing our ice,
telling us to make ourselves at home.
A grey-haired guy said he
owned the island. Owned it.
And I'd have hated him for it
if I wasn't so smiling and warm
and loving every damn thing.
And he probably thought us
a high buncha beatniks
but hey, we had ice.

Looking out at still dark water
at light-dot houses lining the bank
and stars and stars and stars,
I noticed dock creak-cracking sounds,
and stars but no moon
—or maybe all the wine—
but I couldn't see, only guessed
that the creak-cracking was
Sally Sorority and Bobby Frat-Boy
having upper-middle-class
pot-and-Rolling-Rock sex
on the dock, hidden dark by cattails
and a fiberglass skiboat
stencil-named *Atta Girl!*
Sally on a towel,
worried about ass-splinters,
worried about her beer breath,

glad for the cover of cattails
casting spooky wavy shadows
on her V-spread rippling thighs.

We re-boarded the boat
and I sat on the driverman's stool,
grabbed his mic,
got on the loudspeaker, hollering
All aboard the USS Poet!
or other such sillies I don't remember
and no one heard anyway,
and I was feeling fine
and nibbling gouda and Kalamata olives
and honeydew cantaloupe hunks
streaked red with berries,
and all of us wanting to be
just there, just now
and the boat—
rumba splosh
rumba splosh
rumba splosh

To George Saunders, if That is Your Name

I cannot find you online—
young art teacher from Ghana
whose face I cannot precisely remember,
but whose name I thought I did.

I am certain I remember your voice, and
feeling chic driving
out of town to the small riverside gallery
that hosted your first solo show.

Two rooms of huge canvases
shouting their colors, exuberant you
beyond chalk on classroom slate.

This was what you had emigrated to do—
not to teach me
and my similar oblivious hundreds.

If I could find you online,
I could prove
to myself that you existed,
that you complimented my
color choices, my imagination, my
perspective.
I could browse your progress,

satisfied that you painted on
despite us, that we
did not steal the life from your love,
that my country kept you,
coaxed your carnival of liquids, your
body silhouetted before your canvases,
having lain yourself open.

Jeanne Calment of France

Did she know who he was—
Van Gogh—
when as a girl she sold him paints,

noting his eyes glazed
like halved oysters in their liquor,

his verdigris skin
like centuries-old copper
or birches rough with lichens,

On her death
age 122, did she still
think of him as she had then—
ugly as sin and
smelling of booze,

tainting her shop like a burnt thing,
producing art like hydrangeas—
brilliant blue in acidic soil?

Phantosmia

(after *Portrait and a Dream,* Jackson Pollock, oil & enamel on canvas, 1953)

The internet says *brain tumor,* or
it's nothing, will disappear soon—
this phantosmia,
this phantom cloud of
cigarette ash smoke smell
surrounding me always.
No one is smoking.

Pollock, in his self-portrait, seems
to dream in charcoal strokes of something burnt,
in black and gray and blacker,
his skin still embered orangey and remembering.

It happened several months ago, too.
The internet says *migraine,*
and I *have* been needing aspirin.

Today's coffee is flavored with my days
waitressing the smoking section.
This toast and ham and eggs taste like
my 1980s Easters in Grandpa's postwar house—
he and dad and all the uncles smoking,
ashing into empty Coke cans.
Three of those men now are ash.

Self-portrait with odor of tar.
Portrait of a woman enshrouded in
nicotine and cinders.

Pollack smoked while he worked.
Maybe gray particles imbedded
in draperies and bedspreads
leeched into his dreams. Maybe

he knew the smoke was
as much his skin as his skin was.

Maybe this smell will never leave me—
is me now. I never smoked.
Swore I'd never marry a smoker like my father,
ash smell wafting off my coat when
I opened my school locker.
Maybe his ghost haunts my nose now,
offended I didn't keep his ashes in a locket
or a vase on the mantel.
I don't have a mantel.
Don't have a fireplace.

Self-portrait enveloped by
that which cannot be verified.
Portrait of a woman running from
invisible fire.

Pollack *must* have ashed
from lip to canvas as he bent, flung
paint toward the floor,
like artists adding cremains to paints
for their portraits of the dead.

The internet says *Parkinson's*
or *chronic sinusitis*.
Portrait of a woman shadowed in soot.

I don't have a chimney.
My backyard grill burns blue gas, not charcoal.
I never light candles.
I have learned not to leave things burning.

Florist Fire

(Sink's Flower Shop, Findlay, OH 8/26/2014)

They say it could have been arson
that took the flower shop that
for eighty-eight years was
tucked a couple blocks off Main St.
in amongst the houses like
one chrysanthemum
in a vase of carnations.

By dawn, the neighbors who had
slept through sirens and shattered
greenhouse glass awoke
to muddied grass and film of ash,
maybe threw open windows
hoping for the scent of
roses and gardenias in the smoke.

Dave I

In the town of 16,000
the man at the coffee shop mic
blues-growled Johnny Cash against
a pre-recorded harmony machine.
He didn't realize he didn't need
fake backups, that the earnest scrunch
of his brow was enough.

Maybe his wife should
kiss him good luck more often
on his balding head
on his way out
the squealing screen door to gigs,
saying he doesn't
need luck anyway.

Maybe his son should brag
to his friends more,
showing them bar flyers,
not knowing what *dollar-drafts* means,
showing-off the one chord Daddy
taught him to drag across
the hollow yawn of his guitar.

An old man in the coffee shop audience
distributes business cards
advertising jingle-writing, song-writing,
certain you'll love what he creates.
Money-back guarantee.
Dave should sing himself
a similar offer.

Dave II

Stormclouds dawdled,
dumping sorrow down on
two June days.
The young bluesman and his guitar
ached into the coffee shop corner stage,

waiting for his wife to call
to say the baby's coming.

Water gurgled down sloping streets
into iron drain grates,
fighting into holes of manhole covers.

The baby would be a girl.
Dave breathed his insides out
into the mic,
wondered if roads to the hospital
would be flooded,
planning a second route,

wondered if the baby would like guitar,
would watch his fingers
pick and strum
like raindrops.

Daylong June Downpour

A red sedan half sunk in brown
highway ditch muck,

woman emerging arms-first from
the window,

tow truck man watching
from rained-on gravel.

Were there startled
snapping turtles?

Did she salvage
her purse?

Is a daughter waiting
at a packed bowling alley?

A husband awaiting
news of dinner?

How long did she wait, sinking
before birthing herself out?

Coney Island

The kids wouldn't hear
that the water

was too cold to swim,
not when it was their first glimpse

of a suggestion
of this old ocean, not when

a hundred others flopped
soaked bodies

waves to sand
to waves. Had I been

born a hundred years ago
I would have brought parasols

to fight lacily against
cloud-misted

July sun. But I was not, so
the boys' shorts are soaked

thigh-high, and my daughter's
dress waist-down. Laughter,

gulls, pop-music loudspeakers
honking cars

and these ancient waves wash the grit
of a day in the city

from our lungs
but with this decade's ruckus.

Reasons to Pull the Car Over on a Narrow Country Highway

1.

The man walked into the straggly strip of tiger lilies and grasses and morning glories—closed now—bordering the roadway and a soybean field, his long-lensed camera raised, strap draped around his neck, relaxed, as if of course he must shoot what it is there in the field he sees.

2.

The woman had watched the car in front of her quaintly straddle the fresh carcass of an orangey cat, but she had not comprehended in time, and rather felt her front left tire squash, and the rear tire skid out a bit with two soft thuds that shivered her spine like a lie to the face, or a nightmare remembered midday. So she stopped, crawled over the passenger seat, left the door wide, lunged, and vomited into the just-plowed-under soil, heaved remorse to the weevils and crickets, as if it was unjust to be nonchalantly alive.

Luck

The old man was short some,
so he bought only
the box of band-aids,
not the cigarettes—
watching the cashier lady's arm
reach them back to
the shelf behind her head.

I knew what sweet smell
would crinkle from the package
when squeezed a little.

Out in the lot
in a rusted red pickup truck,
he scratched at a lotto ticket,
and I wondered where
his bleeding was.

Beta Fish

Stopping at the pet store for
a last-minute Christmas gift
for my son—
solitary fish
for a fourteen-year-old so often
alone in his room,
Delicate creature friend,
blue as nebulae.

An old woman
wandered the parking lot
with a snow shovel,
offering work.
I remembered
she had knocked at my house
mid-November
with a rake, but too late—
weeds and leaves dead and blown gone.
I had given her a five-dollar bill and
goodbye through a barely-opened door.

Now, with the bagged fish
in my car's cupholder,
I drove beside her,
handed her a twenty,
her eyes panicked blue as a Beta's fins,
What can I do? she hoisted her shovel.
Just have a nice Christmas.

I drove, guilty-ill in my gut for
my flicker of pride in giving,
wishing I had asked her name,
had asked

why she wore only one glove,
had given her mine.

The fish would be
living decoration on my son's desk—
blue as August mornings
and lap pools,
blue as stiff new Levis,

He'll be proud when he
remembers to feed it.

The Argyle Building Fire

(Findlay, OH 2/23/2012)

The downtown apartment-dwellers fled
black smoke in cold pre-dawn dark.
Fire engine waters stormed from
the top floor down, pouring debris—
Coke cans, soggy cardboard, charred hunks of
hundred-twenty-two-year-old wood and plaster,
and scummed hypodermic needles—
all waterfalling down the narrow stairwell
to the Main St. sidewalk.
Dawn's blue light revealed ashy damage,
the filth flushed out, folks
scattered to the Red Cross Shelter,
to cousins' couches and rugs,
to different similar brick-and-sandstone cracks.

The neighboring bakery, wine shop
hair salon, and deli all
wonder who had lived in those high rooms,
having known only occasional voices—
the bass-booming man and snare-drum woman
thumping, hollering nightly wall to wall.
Or the children running, shrieking in the hallway,
street-level ears tilted upward,
determining the shrieks were from play.
Or the weekly firm pronouncement of policemen
pounding fists on doors.

The voices the washed-out shopkeepers
remember, now that it was over
and the lease is still due despite

mopping the ruin of waterlogged inventory.
The voices they remember now—
like midday remembering a dog who
had howled them awake the midnight before,
and, stumbling to the window,
peering green lawn to greener-still lawn,
not seeing who it was had howled.

Without Blue

An article says several ancient languages
had no word for the color blue
until long after other colors,
and that without a name
there was reason to believe they didn't
see the color blue.

The way grass is just *grass,*
the blades remaining nameless.
The way the ocean is just *ocean*
without naming each clear droplet.

The way people streaming by in the airport,
are just *crowd,* are unidentified *them,*
and thus the shock of seeing someone there
whose name you know—
the *Molly!* glowing against so many *thems.*

Was it because those ancient cultures
already had named blue *sky,* blue *sea—*
those bluest, broadest, and most vital blues?

The way reading the story of
an Ethiopian girl, named *Liat,*
scooping her family's daily water
from a stream with a clay pot,
makes us see that water, *Liat's* water
Liat's hands in brown water.
The water is not blue.
The girl is not blue.
But, once finally named,
we can become each other's *blue—*
see each other.

I've Never Been to Cleveland

but I know it is not Toledo.
Has the vast Lake Erie shoreline
instead of the mere Maumee River,
so I have to imagine not being able
to see the other side,
to watch gulls alight and soar,
never knowing how far 'til they land.

I know it is not Sandusky—
searching inside itself for why it deserves
its bluegreen Lake Erie shoreline
instead of just Plum Creek,
Mills Creek, Pipe Creek.
And it doesn't hold the headstones of
all those dead men of my blood.

It's certainly not Findlay,
where I ended-up somehow
amongst all these other enders-up
lodged contentedly midway
up Ohio's west coast, with just
the Blanchard River and
a dozen floody little brother creeks.

Cleveland can't be like landlocked Lima,
hovering amongst farmfields,
though it shares railroads and refineries,
football fans draped brown and orange
regardless of whether they're on
the ninth hole or the factory line.

If I someday visit Cleveland—
not just Avon Lake again or
winging through on I-90—
but if I should stay a while,
I do imagine it feeling like kin, like
the home of a cousin with the same
family reunion photo framed on an end table,
the same recipe for potluck cheesy-potatoes,
the same factory smoke like the perfume
of a stranger wafting past in a crowd that
makes you turn sharply around
with anticipation of a hug,
and ask the breeze, "Aunt Susan?"

To the Singer Boy

The near-empty downtown warehouse bar feels
more like home to me tonight because
I've had enough of this love shit.

It's like when you—
the one good singer at tonight's sad open-mic—
finished your set, and the air slumped
cold like clay across the shoulders of the room,
and I hated you for
having been willing to be so beautiful.

You look like you're in high-school and afraid,
despite how perfectly you strum and sing
into shadowed oak. Someone
should tell you not to be. Should tell you to
have a bourbon with the middle-aged lady
at the far end of the glossy wood bar
and both be not afraid anymore together.

Earlier my younger sister admitted she had been afraid
of my leftover high-school shadow,
but it was, maybe, a shadow she
had cast with her own hands and
a bare bulb onto her bedroom wall.
It's doubtful anyone there noticed I left its halls,
or noticed when I still slouched at its desks,
whispered behind its typewriters,
nibbled flaccid green beans at its Formica tables.

High-school taught me to love boys like you
and to be forgotten by boys like you—
lessons I didn't absorb as readily as
World History or Geometry.
All those beheaded queens and obtuse angles had
practical applications after all.
I have to leave soon because no one knows
I am here nor will notice when I'm gone.
It's not like anyone stays here forever, right?

You're on stage again with an amp you don't need,
and I want tell you to turn it off because
it's untrue and loud, and right now
I could use some dark real whispers.

This Time

(Findlay, OH 4/21/2016)

This time
the fire began on the third floor
and was likely arson.
This time a man jumped from up there
and all the bystanders paused, at first, in shock
then rushed to the brokenness on the sidewalk,
the nurse there doing what she could.
This time it was spring
and warm windless drizzle helped a little.
There will always be these
men willing to jump.
There will always be women hovering over,
doing what they can.

To the Roofers

An isolated May hailstorm
ping-ponged ice balls through car windshields,
obliterated rose bushes, cracked mailboxes,
street signs, and swingset slides.
And all summer-long that half-hour storm has
brought you men from, I imagine, several counties—
scores of tanned-skin teams hammering,
the curbsides clogged with trucks and
dumpster bins and tow-behind trailers
heaped with asphalt shingles.

You perch atop steep peaks,
scrape and shave debris to tarps below
draped over hedge-rows, enjoying
the necessary destruction,
the smoothed, readied surface in your wake.
You unroll sheets of black tarpaper,
sealing with slamming thumps of your gun,
the repeated reverb rumbling
the bones of your arms, your deltoids.
You arrange the stiff, glimmery shingles,
your keen eyes conscious of correct overlapment,
pleased by the perfection of pattern,
the time of day measured in covered square-footage.

The neighborhood wives ogle from windows,
standing far enough inside to be inconspicuous,
fanning their flushed faces with insurance checks.
They hope the pool of skilled men
is not stretched too thin.
They compare crews, hoping
the thumping above their own heads is from
the brightest of the hammer-swingers,
that theirs are the men who

loved Spirograph as children and Erector sets.
For their next-door neighbors, they prefer
the strongest of your lot, overheating, peeling
damp shirts from your planked backs,
hair a bit longer and looser than their husbands',
bending lithe legs to reach for a Coke.
You tower from precarious peaks like
the bronze statue of a city's founder atop
its town hall—a city founded upon the values of
musculature, sweat, and denim shorts.

To the Fellow Airport Travelers

I scan your faces, determining
which are the weary, headed
home to familiar sheets,

which are the exuberant out-bounders,
hop-scotching themselves away from
everyday encumbrances.

We soar to deliberate towns
with books for the interim,
tiny bottles of lotion, boarding passes,

we pull behind us garments we have chosen
for the presentation of our bodies
to foreign places—

this is who I am
beneath new skies,
out from under the roofs of the typical.

Los Angeles Hotel Breakfast

An Italian woman mumbles
around a mouthful of Belgian waffle.

Four film-lovely Japanese girls
titter over the toaster's unfamiliar dials,
frantic to free their rapidly-darkening
slices of wheat.

A father coos French into his
toddler daughter's ear,
feeds her sips of glassy juice.

Two broad men in black t-shirts
grimace the bleak consonants of
eastern Europe at each other's shorn heads,
cereal milk dripping
from their raised spoons.

The sun will coax us all out to LA's
discombobulated streets.
Our necks will crane upward
toward billboards in rotation,
downward to grimy, embossed stars,
gasping at glimpses of beauties
who may or may not be famous,
fingers sticky with juice of
ever-present fruits
tumbling from streetside markets
and carts like heaps of toys
in the playroom of a spoiled child.

Of Oils

1.

Mouse-girl in the back of the classroom
whose hairs conglomerated in striations,
enunciating the tufts'
growth patterns—like a field
of soil, freshly-tilled and
inoculated with rows of unseen seeds.

2.

Olives were plucked and pressed
to meld my panful of
chopped onion and garlic,
translucening their cellulose
with celery, carrot in golden sluice,
as if the olives—
who could not avoid their own demise—
will accomplice
fellow vegetables' slow sweat.

3.

Iridescent swirls floating
on parking-lot puddles.
Retired from the work of slicking
cars' gears and ball bearings,
left now to drift and glimmer
momentarily—sinking back into black
asphalt nooks when the sun
completes its work of evaporation.

4.

My fingertips smell of tangerine peels,
the citrus oils dense as chrism,
blessing the nailbeds
with winter sweetness.
Perhaps the wisemen, instead of myrrh,
could have bestowed upon the babe
an ark of oranges.

5.

I rub mentholated ointment
on my son's chest—
like the hull of a ship-in-a-bottle.
The slickness smells blue as
peeks of January sky between
swells of snowcloud.
The iced-whiskey vapor will
expand alveoli, soothe mucosa,
bring sleep. It will.

6.

We revive February feet with
smeared petroleum
jelly at bedtime and
sheaths of serious wool socks.
The petrolatum knows
to be sucked by crusted whorls,
ooze into crevasses the way
snowmelt seeks the earth's core.

7.

It is both miracle and sin—
the cinnamon and butter in
frivolous veins
through the breadloaf,
preventing the dough from
adhering to itself,
refusing to be absorbed into the dough,
maintaining sweet selfness,
like the best kind of wife.

Spinal Fusion

(for my sister)

It's a lot to ask a woman
        to agree to lie back on a gurney,
        fall asleep through the veins,
and trust the surgeon to
        slice her belly, remove
            the soft obstacles curled there
            for thirty-five years,
trust him to dive his tools and
        hunk of a deadman's bone
        in behind her aorta, throbbing
            the fuel of all of her
and shim her two vertebrae who
        have crushed each other
the deadbone bit like Sister Bernadette wedging
        apart two eight-graders
            slow dancing high-school close,
        because there's no telling how wrongly
            the two might choose to fuse.
It's a lot to ask a woman
        to decide how much pain
            she's willing to claim as her self,
how often she's willing to stay in bed
        because her legs refuse to listen,
to decide that being filleted in fluorescent light
        is her best option,
signing-off on being turned inside-out,
deciding beforehand who should keep her cats
        and where to be buried
            should the surgeon fail at
            the putting-back-in.

It's a lot to ask a team of strangers
        to love her organs
                like she didn't realize she did herself,
      enough to return them snugly
            to their slick homes,
     to love her dancer's spine
             like she remembers having loved it,
                  twisting as streams do.

To the Woman in the Fruit Factory Photo

You glove the fruits
as they roll, glossed,
along the rubber conveyor.

I do not know what they are, nor
which I should select if prompted—
the chartreuse
or those blushed coral,
ashamed of their own ripeness.

Why do you reach for
the fruit you do now?
To reject it—flawed—
or because it represents the ideal?
Or to pocket it in your apron—
glancing first over your shoulders—
for your youngest daughter?
Are they her favorite?

Those fruits you sort—
might someone melt them into jam,
or apply their juice to open wounds,
or steep their seeds for tea
to calm viruses of the chest?

What becomes of your hours
of attentive selection?
Of the hairs loosed from
your ponytail to the concrete floor?

What else do you reach for
with gloved fingertips,
decide the value of,
imagining the taste its rind implies
as it scrolls by your eyes
in an endless tumble?

Watermelon Seeds

(for Don McKivett)

It has been a week's-worth of sticky June—
the sky glowering, threatening to rumble a shower,
as if it's pissed-off, maybe at some offhand comment
somebody made, but it won't just come out and
holler and stomp and say it's angry.

I bake cinnamon bread and soak a pot of chicken soup,
confusing my sweaty skin—cooking like October
and somebody's coming home for supper.

But heat or no heat, I need to keep busy.
The onions get to my eyes, and I wonder
if Don liked his chicken soup thick,
clouded with dumplings pale and soft as
a fat mama's arms around your ribcage,

or more Cubano—cilantro, yucca,
plantains like some golden archipelago,
squeeze of lime at the table.

Hell, he might have been vegetarian.

I chop straight through a watermelon,
the halves sighing away
from each other like disgruntled lovers,

and I wonder if Don liked watermelon—
sucking triangle wedges on a beach with
a sweating bottle of beer,
spitting black seeds
off to his left in the sand, laughing.

And maybe Don's up there in Heaven doing just that.
Spitoo! go the melon seeds,
sipping his beer
and goofin in the sun with his mother and brothers
and John Swaile and Kerouac and
all the chickens he never ate but other folks did,
and he's got stories to get em all rollin.

My watermelon has a dark, muggy-looking
vein of over-ripe flesh running through it,
bordering on fermented,

and I cry, wiping juicy fists across my eyes,
thinking, why in God's Green
does something so joyful, lovely,
have to be ruined.

June Cherry-Picking Pantoum

drops of last night's thundershowers sprinkle my calves
the first fruits toll in the colander like churchbells
communion of June drops and juice on fingertips
leaves tickle my thighs, or possibly a spider

the first fruits toll in the colander like churchbells
leaves curled like palms, prone, demonstrating innocence
leaves tickle my thighs, or possibly a spider
I resign myself to spiders, earwigs, inchworms

leaves curled like palms, prone, demonstrating innocence
Eve must have faced insects in her virgin apple
I resign myself to spiders, earwigs, inchworms
the worm warning *no* as the serpent urges *yes*

Eve must have faced insects in her virgin apple
I take just enough bursting redness for today
the worm warning *no* as the serpent urges *yes*
some fruits ruptured from waiting too long to be plucked

I take just enough bursting redness for today
drops of last night's thundershowers sprinkle my calves
some fruits ruptured from waiting too long to be plucked
communion of June drops and juice on fingertips

To the Tongue

Lapping, from your start,
at amniotic fluid,
you educate yourself on
sriracha and sugar,
like a warning.
Later, you suckle for life,
in sync with breathing,
or asleep in milky dreams.
You study grown, hidden
tongues to imitate language—
slips of millimeters
forward transforming
oven to *lovely,*
a push of breath
turning *link* to *think.*
You star in whistles,
hover idle for laughter,
suck the salt of blood
from insignificant wounds.
You create, of chewing,
a sensory joy,
commanding brains to
learn and savor
earth and its creatures
through oregano, scallops,
blackberries or tomato.
Your gymnastics can
sublimate the iciest lips,
can will nerve endings
to samba and swirl
like cobras from baskets.
You, a muscled
soul, kindling.

Cycles

The huge hoppers of
busted glass funk the air
surrounding the recycling center
with faint brine like
the lingering of sex on skin.

I hoist my bin of wine
bottles into other greens,
clears of olives and gin
into clears, browns into
malty beers and salty soy.

The clattering releases
sugars, yeasts and vinegars,
disparate ferments oozing
in translucent shatter, juices
awaiting transmutation.

Wasted

(the Heaven Hill Distillery fire, 11/7/1996)

Foxes smelled the burning oak
and alcohol before the humans did—
the way you know an unseen lake is near
by scent of its evaporation.

Barrel by barrel explosions,
ninety-thousand bungs launched
skyward, sideward
as alcohol realized its
ancillary potential—fuel—burning
ricks and lawn instead of throats.

Dazed crows dodged
blast-flung staves and
three-hundred-foot flames,
saw rivers of blazing
bourbon through black plumes.

Five, seven, twenty years of resting labor,
of commitment to creation that's at least
a five-years wait to reap—like planting
a peach orchard or asparagus patch—
all wasted downhill like lava flows
in sixty-mile-per-hour wind.

Corn vapors remembered
having been born of nearby fields
and to fields they shall return.
The air boozy for miles—
the angels taking more than their fair share,
the devil's cut cindered to smoky rubble.

Bluegill in creeks had
hardly oxygen enough after
the hot whiskey flood,
their gills rinsed in sugary oak,
above, buzzards riding
updrafts of caramel.

Never Having Tasted a Hot-Fudge Sundae

you have missed the blue shiver
sliding from the world outside
into your organs, your blood.

The fudge like a clean towel
wrapping pool-chilled shoulders,
disappearing like breeze the same ninety-degrees
as the still air, such that it riffles your hair
like invisible ghosts of August.

You haven't crunched
brittle, undefinable nuts—not almonds nor pecans—
but simply *nut topping*
suspended in the creamy love,
surprising teeth with metallic tingles,
like church bells through autumn fog.

You haven't scraped a Styrofoam cup
with a plastic spoon, shaving black-brown from white,
licking it off the spoon turned upside-down
against your tongue tip.

Haven't felt sun singeing your hairline,
mown grass under bare feet.

A Taste for Salt

His soups never
have enough salt,
Mom grumbled with the shaker.
It's never the same
trying to add it
afterward.

I thought
she could have just thought this.
Could have
sipped her disappointment down
without sprinkling it into
my bowl too.

Thirty years later,
her blood pressure is high—
as it maybe always was—
her body swollen like a hot sea,
and I perpetually
over-salt my pots-full.

To the Four People in the Theater Seats in Front of Me

You smell like you just
came from a restaurant—

complimentary mini bread
loaves sliced on wooden boards

and buttered, dense crusts torn
and passed hand to hand.

There must be
crumbs in your hair, rosemary

breath, and that
one last

sip as you rose—*oh, we*
should get going—

of crushed-ice water cooling garlic
throats and balsamic.

Lunch Bag

Across from me, not trying, I can see
the topography of his scrotum, mushed
just to the left of his khakis' inseam.
I wonder why it sagged to that side, rushed
to choose just at the moment of sitting.
I wish the broad, tan bulge could not be seen,
am ashamed for him that he, unwitting,
scribbles his blue notepad, dunking his tea
bag unaware that anyone with eyes
despite not wanting to, readily can
approximate the volume and the size
of his restrained scrotal sack—larger than
a pickled egg, smaller than a steaming
meatball sub, larger than a tangerine.

Poet with a Comb-over

How can someone as observant as you,
whose lifetime is spent concluding
motive behind the subtlest of motions—
like whether the bird grew his feathers blue
to feel kin to sky, or whether
the young girl released her grip
on her green balloon because its light bobbing
on her wrist mocked her, reminded her
she had no choice but be grounded—

how can you not see that
those hairs sprung from your left temple—
grown, I must assume, a foot long now,
to stretch up and across the dome of
your otherwise well-aged skull,
and on down the right side—
those hairs are being asked to perform
an unnatural duty?

Hair's desire is to flow
lazily downward, like rivers.
Have you never noticed—
in the years of your eyes' intent looking,
translating the world through to your pen,
finding beauty in the world with
its flaws all splayed and bare—
have you never noticed
that hair is a gravitational thing,
susceptible to breeze and sex and dancing?

Did no lover ever ask—
after a bath, as the left side hung free,
dripping your left shoulder, biceps,
the gleaming, just-cleaned head-skin
tautly damp and aired—
ask to cut it for you?
Offer to stroke it smooth, relax it,
snip—*there now, it's over, breathe.*

To the Toy Stuffed Animal Pile

In the dark basement, you are
tumbled in entangled mounds of
candy-colored, furry limbs
and plastic noses, piled high
in two laundry baskets,
glassy, black eyes transfixed,
glinting here and there within
the throng of fuzz and fluff.
At least you can soothe each other,
warmed by your mass
like penguins, but without rotation
from the cool outer edges of the huddle
to the middle's drowsy constriction.
It must be enough for you
until the day you all are overturned
in a breathy heap to the carpet,
rummaged and stroked and
swum through, lain upon,
toted in purses, and maybe
just maybe, welcomed into bed,
where body heat and smooth sheets
warm your marble eyes to tears.
Where you stare the night through at
chinks of moonlight on walls,
at a child's lax, dreaming face with
her eyes deliciously closed.

What Was Taken in Ohio Last Night

(1/23/2016)

The Findlay, Main Street pawn shop had moved
its crates of watches, guitars, and cubic zirconias
a block north after a seven-years-ago fire,
moved north again after a half-dozen
Blanchard River floods soaked the floors.
Smaller space but rent cheap enough
to keep on going a while, until
last night's fire in the upper apartments
meant more smoke and cold floods—
this time from the ceilings down.

Last night ambulance lights flashed in
my daughter's window, her awake already,
throbbing from foot surgery—
pulsing pain in lonely dark.
It was as though the winter-bundled men
had come to take her.
Instead they took the old man from the house
across the street on a stretcher again,
his younger wife shivering on the porch—
face flashed red-black-red-black-red.

In one of the Findlay Main Street apartments
our friend Rabbit was showering when firemen
broke down his door like in movies,
shouting fire and smoke, forcing him wet outside
where ice drooped from smoky windows like
dogs' frozen tongues, where he saw the glow that
had been licking above him and his neighbors.

He took nothing—not even the photos, books or
coin collection salvaged from his
dead mother's home two months before.

The Toledo pastor who opens his kitchen
and coffee tables for community dinners,
who drives a mobile medical clinic van
into forgotten neighborhoods on days off,
whose previous house burned down
to foundation block four years ago—
last night fire came for him again,
taking his two dogs, taking his possessions,
leaving only a shelf of smoky books
and prayers readily given and given.

Soot

When the demo crew went to work
on the burnt-out building,
the scent of soot was released
upon Main Street like spores,
reminding drivers-by of
a century of bones between brick walls.

The soot held the sweat of the pawn shop
owner, waking, haunted by
stories in his storefront below.
The fur of twelve cats fed that one last
time by the body of the old lady herself.
The spit of a black couple evicted
for walking too hard on their own floors.
The cigarette smoke, burnt toast
smack grit, Aqua Net,
Pine-Sol, Love's Baby Soft,
bong smoke, bacon grease.

Trucks smashed and rumbled heaps into
other trucks that rumbled it all away—
to where I don't know—but soot
lingers there awaiting scrubbing
and a second chance at
holding somethings together.

The Table

There was a table,
in the small bright dining room of a small bright house,
where she placed a box of crackers—

exotic crackers from a discount bin at the discount store,
crackers with foreign writing and a photograph of
the crackers' hope to be topped with
caviar, minced onion, and full moons of boiled egg.

Instead someone else brought two cans of sardines
for the crackers, for the table.

And someone brought three waxy green apples
crisp enough the knife needed leaning on,
slamming down to the board, the table shuddering.

And someone brought red wine—
no matter it was cheap and caustic, there was plenty.

And they all brought poems to scribble,
story-tell, and dismiss in their brilliance.

Sometimes in her dreams she's eating crackers at that table.
The zinfandel swallows her tongue.
She brushes crumbs from her lip, her lap,
falling gently to the floor.

Food for the Dead

(for John Swaile)

Dressing in black for you and for those
you've left—in no need of color today—
I prepare to cook some food you'll never eat,
but just the rest of us—
the taste on our tongues, you on our brains.
I wonder what to feed
those left behind a dead man.
What flavors should accompany
our recitation of your poems,
our remembrance of your laugh, your sweat,
your anxious stroking of hair from your brow,
with voice booming sweetly?

I remember the last food you made for me:
a white brick of cream cheese,
softened a bit from the warm car ride,
plopped from its silver wrapper
to an oval yellow platter,
topped with a jar's-worth of jalapeno jelly—
wet green as any summer.
It isn't hot, you assured me,
scraping a glob with a butter knife
onto a golden cracker.
It's sweet, you said, chewing
and your lips wouldn't lie, would they?
And someone handed me
a glass of wine I hadn't asked for,
and someone else read a poem,
and you held up a finger which meant,
wait for me to swallow;

I have something I must say.
And you scooped me a cracker—
glistening green swirled with creamy white,
like jewels in snow,
and I shoved it, whole, into my mouth,
and damn if it wasn't sweet after all.

Roasting Turkey for Friends

Drippings crackle brown to the roasting pan
and the house is gauzed with rosemary smoke.
The beast's neck and gizzards poach in celery,
sage and an onion's outermost white cloak.
Outside, January bombasts itself
against the windows and kowtowing shrubs.
As a girl I would wake Thanksgiving late
morning at my grandparents' quiet house
to the same sizzle, bake and boil, to the
oiled mechanisms of seasonal feast,
the small bathroom, with its ever-closed door,
the only room in the house left unsmoked
and cool with fogged window and sweet soap—like
stepping into a cardinal's startled heart.

Words to Speak in the Dark

Some folks at the poet's wake read his poetry
or poems inspired by him.
But others—while we all strained to hear
over chatter and spasming fans on
the downtown Toledo bar's tin ceiling,
while we nibbled crackers and brownies
and sipped draft beer, while we strained to see
our food on plastic spoons in the dark wood room—
some other people simply read their own poems
because the mic was there, because they enjoyed
being silhouetted against the slim flash of window.
The poet had been a knitter, and some guests wore
his bright, loose scarves and pommed hats
as they nodded response to the mic,
as they sliced the lemon pound cake.
The poet had been a social worker,
giving one poet the right, she thought,
to announce from her perch at the mic,
And here's a poem about sexual harassment…

Days earlier, some friends had a barbecue,
one of many that night in tiny Carey, OH,
renowned for its shrine to the Virgin Mary.
She-of-so-many-names is, in that town,
Our Lady of Consolation, and she beckons
annual pilgrims from miles and miles.
As the townsfolk's charcoal cools,
they watch from porches as
thousands of travelers flow, in twilight,
toward Main Street, toward the shrine, with
slim white candles pierced through paper cups.
White-cloaked priests and altar-boys
billow from the church, hefting a four-foot
statue of the bejeweled Virgin.

The flock follows with its candles,
filling Main Street and its front lawns,
the microphoned priest reciting
the series of prayers of the rosary beads,
the thrum of the crowd repeating words memorized
in the languages of their childhood,
pinching each strung bead in succession,
mesmerized by the Lady.

In a dark corner of the bar wake,
I leaned on my husband's shoulder,
wished I had known the poet better,
wished he had a book that I could, now,
recite from, filling the dim air with him,
diminishing the acquaintances dabbing their
eyes with their own scrawled poems.
I forked the cake on my paper plate,
disappointed I had not collected more of his poems,
that I have not shared more copies of mine
with my someday mourners.

Against the candled crowd of pilgrims hailing Mary,
my husband and I walked to our car.
I could not resist mumbling along with
what I could recall of the prayers of my youth.
The undulating procession of pray-ers glowed toward
a park at the end of Main Street,
for mass at the foot of the jeweled statue of
Our Lady of Consolation. We, instead,
rode the highway home to our children,
whispering together behind windows,
bright against the night.

The poet had written, years back, a poem
sensing he might die young. Perhaps he was
already ill then, words paddling fast
in a panicked rush toward life's liquid surface.
In the words of his poem I can smell
the woodsmoke of his suspicion that
the world he would someday leave behind
just might pay too much attention to
the cheese dip, and to what's on tap.
I recognized his resignation—to death,
to the living that would continue
in a lighted mass of mumbling bodies behind him.
I hadn't the strength to read it at his wake—
because I could not admit his possibility for myself.
There were many other words to speak in the dark,
to those I love, and to my own skin—
words I would mean entirely more,
words of little consolation.

To the Poets

Like Mary Oliver
wandering her woods
    gathering mushrooms
    fish and berries
        like a black bear
    gathering language
    in which to house herself—
        sumac walls and
        mayapple carpet,

I forage
for what I need
    among you,
stanzas of sustenance
swelled with
    the juice of what it means
        to have been living.

Banana Aubade

I awoke, having slept on the couch, my cheek
no doubt pocked with pillow texture.
And before I registered even the time
as judged by light's blue between drape seams,
and before my tongue had time to crave
coffee's acids on its buds,
I smelled the bananas—

exquisitely ripe.
My body actually sought them out,
finding them nestled in their blue glass bowl.
Their daintily freckled skins
like a child's summer cheeks,
blushed bronze enough to enrichen the
gaudy yellow of rawness.

They'd roused me with their
buttered orchid scent
like sweet liquor in the dark air,
like a sunrise, those sirens
begging to be split, whispering sweetly,
their skin to mine, *today.*

About the Author

Kerry Trautman lives in smalltown Ohio and is a founder and admin of ToledoPoet.com and the "Toledo Poetry Museum" page on Facebook. Kerry participates in poetry readings and events such as Artomatic 419, 100-Thousand Poets for Change, Poetry Out Loud, Back to Jack, and the Columbus Arts Festival. Her poetry and short fiction have appeared in various print and online literary journals, including *Midwestern Gothic, Alimentum, The Coe Review, Think Journal, Paper & Ink, Naugatuck River Review,* and *Free State Review.* Kerry's poetry has also appeared in anthologies such as *Mourning Sickness* (Omniarts 2008), *Journey to Crone* (Chuffed Buff Books 2013), and *Delirious: a Poetic Celebration of Prince* (NightBallet Press 2016). Her poetry chapbooks are *Things That Come in Boxes* (King Craft Press 2012) *To Have Hoped* (Finishing Line Press 2015) and *Artifacts* (NightBallet Press 2017).